ROLLS-ROYCE

GEORGE BISHOP

Designed by
PHILIP CLUCAS MSIAD

Produced by
TED SMART and **DAVID GIBBON**

CRESCENT BOOKS
NEW YORK

FOREWORD

In 1907 an event took place which clearly established the Rolls-Royce motor car in the forefront of the motoring scene. A 40/50 hp model, designed by Henry Royce and named the Silver Ghost, succeeded in completing 15,000 miles without an involuntary stop – a feat which at that time was more than double the then existing world record.

The Silver Ghost series was given the accolade 'The Best Car in the World' by the motoring press of the time and in this account of Rolls-Royce history, George Bishop describes how the company has striven over the years to maintain its unique reputation.

Henry Royce's motto "Whatsoever is Rightly Done, However Humble is Noble" became the guiding philosophy for generations of engineers from the earliest days to the present. The meticulous attention to detail in engineering, manufacture and design which he insisted upon is evident in each successive model produced by the company as are the qualities of silence, reliability and, as the large number of older models still running testify, longevity.

I, and my present team of engineers at Crewe are devoted to the pursuit of perfection and we are confident that the current Silver Spirit, Corniche and Camargue cars will be worthy successors to the long tradition established by Rolls-Royce. I will leave it to readers to determine for themselves how we at Crewe have succeeded over the years in the face of changes in social and economic conditions.

George Fenn

GEORGE FENN
Managing Director
Rolls-Royce Motors Limited, Crewe.

Top picture shows one of the most handsome RR models, the Corniche Convertible of 1978, first introduced in 1971. The company call this model 'the ultimate personal Rolls-Royce'. Bodies are built by Mulliner Park Ward. Bottom shot shows the company's original Silver Ghost (left) with a modern two-door Camargue coupé, styled by Pininfarina of Turin and first introduced in 1975. It is the biggest and heaviest RR and a full five-seater, but not the prettiest of shapes. The Camargue was the first RR to be fitted with fully automatic air-conditioning.

ROLLS AND ROYCE

(1) The first Royce car, the 1904 two-cylinder, was in fact the second machine built, for Royce's partner Ernest Claremont. (2) Sir Henry Royce with a rarely-seen smile on his face. (3) Another example of the first model of 1904, with ten horsepower two-cylinder engine, and in this case a two-seater body. The engine was of 1800 cc and total cost of the car was about £400. (4) This Silver Ghost of 1907

has survived 75 years and is still a sweet runner. Known officially as the 40/50, the model was in production for 18 years, a total of 7,800 examples having been made. (5) This 1912 40/50 or Silver Ghost has a Roi des Belges style body of the type popularised by the King of the Belgians, who took an interest in motor sport in the early days of motoring.

1
2
3

4

Although arguments will rage as to whether the Rolls-Royce is indeed the best car in the world, there can be no question that Royce, the engineer, always built his cars to the highest standards, even before he became connected with Rolls, the salesman. It is somewhat ironical that although Royce designed and built the cars, the Rolls name was perpetuated in his creations.

Frederick Henry Royce was born on March 27, 1863 at Awalton near Peterborough, the son of a flour miller whose business had failed. Starting at an early age, his first jobs included selling newspapers and working as a telegraph boy, before he became apprenticed to the Great

Northern Railway, his fees being paid by his aunt. Financial problems terminated his training prematurely, and he was forced to take up employment with a firm of toolmakers. The spare time from this 54 hour a week job was spent studying electrical engineering, and led him to join an electrical company, prior to founding his own electrical manufacturing concern in Manchester, with £20 capital, and a partner.

Royce's first car was a French De Dion quadricycle, a crude machine which he replaced in 1903 with another French model, a secondhand two cylinder Decauville. It was rough and noisy, and Royce, deciding he could improve on the design, built three two-cylinder cars in 1904, which although not a commercial success, were superior to the French original.

Charles Stewart Rolls, third son of Lord Llangattock, ran a successful business selling horseless carriages to the nobility and gentry. He too had experienced the faults of early French cars, having owned a Peugeot. Trading as C.S. Rolls & Co. in London's West End, he heard of Henry Royce's new machine, and arranged a meeting with him at the Midland Hotel in Manchester. The resultant partnership gave Rolls exclusive selling rights to the Royce car.

Royce produced five different cars: a 10 horsepower, another with similar chassis and engine, a 15 and 20 horsepower, and a 30 horsepower six-cylinder model for the Paris show held in the December of 1904. That same month, the two men agreed that the cars would henceforth

factory for ever, and worked from the drawing offices in one of his two homes; one at Canadel-sur-Mer on the French Riviera and the other at West Wittering on the Sussex coast. His wife left him soon after, and his nurse, Ethel Aubin, sustained the great man, a semi-invalid from then on, until his death on April 22, 1933. Legend has it that the colour of the enamel backing on the Rolls-Royce badge was changed from red to black because of his death, but the truth is that he had decided on the change a month earlier, believing the red to clash with some of the colour finishes being used by coachbuilders. Up to 1949 Rolls sold only chassis, the bodies being supplied by coachbuilders.

The distinctive Rolls radiator was designed by Royce in the early days, and although it appears to consist of flat surfaces, it is in fact made up of slightly convex ones, making it much more difficult and expensive

5

be made and sold as the Rolls-Royce. The legend had begun.

The third man in the partnership, universally known as the hyphen in Rolls-Royce, was Claude Johnson, first secretary of the Royal Automobile Club, a shrewd businessman and publicist who married the genius of Royce, the perfectionist engineer, to the sales skills of the aristocratic Rolls. As well as being a keen motorist and racing driver, Rolls was a pioneering aviator, making the first return crossing of the English Channel. He was killed at a flying display in Bournemouth on July 12, 1910.

It was only a year later that Royce, ill from overwork, left his

to manufacture. Royce, however, always did things in what he considered to be the right way, irrespective of cost, even in the early 1900s when he had trouble finding his men's wages at the end of the week.

Rolls had helped the infant company through successful competition in motor-racing, in which the company itself was involved for the first and last time, when Charles Rolls ran in the T.T. This was in 1905, when Rolls wrecked his gearbox while trying to get back into gear, having coasted down a hill. Of course he blamed someone else. Charles Rolls also took two cars on a record attempt to Monte Carlo and back.

ROLLS AND ROYCE

(1) One of the three surviving ten horsepower two-cylinder models of 1905, owned by the company, with open four-seater coachwork. (2) The Hon. Charles Rolls in what he called his 'balloon car'. He was a hot-air balloon enthusiast and flier as well as motorist. It is a 1908 40/50 model, with one-off two-seater bodywork and wire wheels, very much in keeping with his sporting image. (3) One of the most sought-after models today, the 'Baby Rolls' or 20 horsepower, in this case with open tourer body. The model can be identified by the horizontal (instead of vertical) radiator

shutters. (4) This handsome 20 Tourer of 1926 has a body by Barker, who were the official works coachbuilders at that time. (5) The Phantom, which succeeded the Ghost, was also known as the 40/50. The illustration shows a fine example of a 1929 two-ton tourer.

He carried two kinds of refreshment: tea for the crew and champagne for himself. He retrieved his good name by winning the 1906 T.T. in the Isle of Man, which included a fuel limitation of 6.5 gallons for the 162 miles, driving the 20 h.p. car, of which the Rolls-Royce company still have a 1905 example.

Johnson, the 'hyphen man', was as active as Charles Rolls in promoting the product. He ran the six-cylinder 30 horsepower car in tough Scottish reliability trials and other competitions. Having discovered its limitations, however, the car was dropped from the range, being succeeded by the Silver Ghost, which remained in production for 18 years.

The Silver Lady mascot, that familiar hallmark of the Roll-Royce, did not appear until 1911. Designed by the painter and sculptor Charles Sykes, it was officially known as the Spirit of Ecstasy. The original version or 'Standing Lady' was seen on the Ghost models, but later, to suit the shape of the modern cars, the 'Kneeling Lady' took over, and this later modified version is the less valuable.

Ultimately, to suit the safety regulations, the lady had to be made to bend over when pushed, and in the current models, disappears into a hole in the radiator shell when brushed against. There has been much speculation as to the identity of the model used for the original Spirit, or Lady.

Proud owners of Rolls-Royce cars are fond of demonstrating a number of tricks, especially with the earlier models. One is to stand a coin on its edge on the bonnet, to show the smoothness and lack of vibration of the engine. Another is to fire the engine without using the starter, simply by moving the advance-and-retard lever, which is sufficient to give a starting spark. Chauffeurs used to like to do this on pre-war machines, but of course the modern models do not have a spark lever.

— CHAPTER TWO —

In 1905 C.S. Rolls & Co of 14 and 15 Conduit Street, London, W.1., where the Rolls-Royce showroom still is today, produced a brochure stating that the Rolls-Royce car 'is manufactured exclusively for C.S. Rolls & Co by Messrs Royce Ltd., of Hulme, Manchester', although the cover of the publication bore the RR logotype exactly as it appears today on the Grecian radiator.

C.S. Rolls also announced that they were now sole agents for Barker Bodies, and that all Rolls-Royce cars would be fitted with these. They advertised the 10 horsepower two-cylinder—even then 'the most silent two-cylinder car in the world'—at £395 with Barker tonneau body. On the 15, 20 and 30 h.p. chassis they were offering, in addition to the tonneau (an open tourer), a detachable hardtop as we would call it now, in shooting-brake form including a windscreen, a luxury missing from the tonneau model.

The most expensive body cost £980, but a hood and lamps were extra, and the lamps were acetylene. As we have seen, three experimental models based on the Decauville were made in 1904, then 16 ten horsepower 1,800 c.c. two-cylinder versions, of which three survive. But in 1905/6 a total of 40 of the four-cylinder Twenty were made, and orders outran production. The machines which ran in the T.T. races were lightened versions of the Twenty, with drilled chassis, wire wheels and a lighter body.

In the 1905 race, over four laps of the 52.75 mile circuit, a second Rolls 20, driven by Percy Northey, finished second, although it had only 18 developed horsepower compared with the twenty produced by the Charles Rolls car, which had a slightly bigger bore. On Northey's best lap he averaged 34.1 mph. In the 1906 race, Rolls won at an average speed of 39.3 mph.

4

5

Charles Rolls said after his victory: 'I had nothing to do but sit there and wait till the car got to the finish. The credit is obviously due to Mr Royce, the designer and builder. I am happy to think it has again been shown how utterly unnecessary it is for a Britisher desiring to purchase a good motor, to spend his money on foreign goods and in the support of foreign workmen, instead of trusting his own country, which is the leading engineering country of the world.'

Charles Rolls was having a little dig at the foreign competition here. In 1899 he had been the first Briton to race abroad, when he ran in the Paris-Boulogne race in a 12 h.p. Panhard, but came last. He then rode

with the famous S.F. Edge on his 16 h.p. Napier in 1900 in the Paris-Toulouse-Paris event, and drove a 60 h.p. Mors in the 1901 Paris-Berlin, and in the Paris-Madrid race of 1903, which was stopped at Bordeaux because of the number of crashes, he failed to finish.

In the 1905 Gordon Bennett race, which was after his meeting with Henry Royce, he drove a British car, a 96 h.p. Wolseley designed by Herbert Austin, to eighth place. Rolls had begun in the motor trade as an importer of French cars, from Lillie Hall in Fulham, which was later to become a Rolls-Royce depot until after the second world war. He had studied engineering at Cambridge after Eton, and originally sold

THE SILVER GHOST

These illustrations show details of the company's own Silver Ghost. The aluminium paintwork and silver plated accessories on this Barker body were the inspiration for the name, which is now applied to all examples. (1) Frontal view of AX 201, with the traditional four-seat open tourer body and two-piece screen. (2) A close-up of the brasswork and black enamel of the 7036 cc engine. The six cylinders were in two blocks of three, with non-detachable cylinder-heads, fed by a single up-draught carburettor. (3) Detail of the massive oil sidelamp, fitted well back close to the screen, which supplemented the forward-mounted headlamps in front of the radiator. (4) This view of the cockpit shows the orthodox pedal layout and simple

instrumentation. (Many early cars had a central throttle pedal.) (5) The wooden wedge holding the clutch out is to stop it sticking when the car is left standing. The central wooden box contains the trembler coil. (6) This photograph of the near-side of the car shows the tool boxes incorporated in the running-boards, platform rear suspension and semi-elliptic front springs. Brakes were internal, expanding on the rear wheels only, and there was also a transmission brake. The 1907 car weighed 3,360 lbs. with a chassis weight of 2,520 lbs. The wheelbase could be either 135.5 or 143.5 inches, and the track was 56 inches. Bodies were built mostly by Barker or Hooper.

—CHAPTER THREE—

Despite the failure of some early models, and discounting the Decauville-based versions, as well as the ten horsepower car that had served as a test rig, the standard of excellence that was to become the Rolls-Royce hallmark was firmly established by 1905.

That year, the three-cylinder 15 horsepower car, with a three-litre engine of three single cylinder blocks, appeared. Only six were made and one is still in existence. Then came the 20, not to be confused with the later Twenty (1922-25) which was a much-loved model if stately and slow, of which 40 were made and sold. This early 20 was a four-litre four-cylinder made at Manchester before the Derby factory was established, from which was derived the lighter sporting model which ran successfully in the two T.T. races. One car is still in existence.

The 30 h.p. six-cylinder was perhaps not a commercial failure as 37 were made and sold (one still survives), but it was dropped by the company even before they embarked on the one-model policy. The two which did not sell were the Legalimit and the landaulet with Invisible Engine, both of which used the first V8 Rolls-Royce engine. Only three examples of the two models were made and none survive.

The Legalimit was a normal-looking car inspired by the pioneer motorist Sir Henry Harmsworth, later Lord Northcliffe, proprietor of the Daily Mail. He suggested that people were fed up with speed and open cars and wanted a petrol-driven equivalent of the then-popular electric town-brougham, with no noise, vibration or smell, and capable of no more than the legal 20 miles an hour.

Royce designed two vehicles: one with no bonnet, known as the Invisible Engine model, and the other with a low bonnet on a two-seater car, both powered by the 3.5 litre V8 side-valve engine.

4

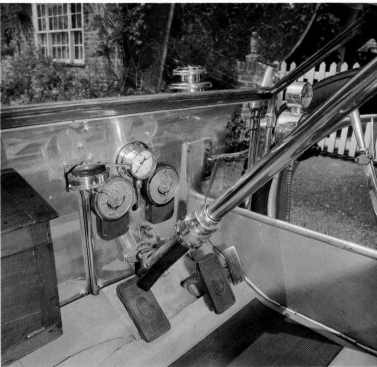

5

6

THE SILVER GHOST

Buyers did not like either car, although Lord Northcliffe was enthusiastic about the smoothness and lack of need for gear-changing; a noisy and difficult task on the early gearboxes.

The unsuccessful V8 did however teach Royce some lessons put to use in the immortal 40/50 or Silver Ghost which followed, firmly establishing the company as a car maker. This car was first shown at the 1906 Olympia motor show in London in November, which coincided with the time chosen to increase the company's capital and to build a new factory. Napier had been successful with the first production six-cylinder, and Royce decided to challenge this form with his own car.

The company had advertised the 30 h.p., now discontinued, as the best car in the world. They now announced the 40/50 as 'the best six-cylinder car in the world', claiming it to be the most graceful, attractive, silent, flexible and smooth-running. The 13th car made was fitted with a Barker body in the style known as *Roi des Belges*. Painted in aluminium and fitted with silver-plated accessories it was called the

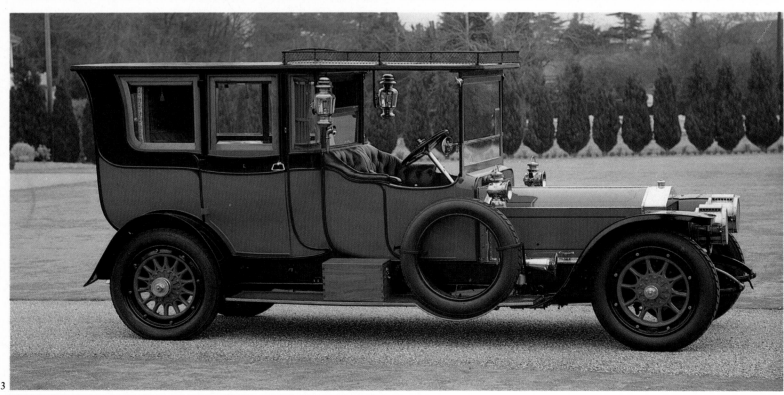

Silver Ghost, a name now given to all 40/50s, although it originally applied to just the one special example, still owned by Rolls-Royce.

The engine of 7,036 c.c. (later 7,428) had pressure lubrication for the crank (most others depended upon the spit-and-hope splash method), and various other refinements. First models had a four-speed gearbox with an overdrive top, and later ones a three-speed. The car could take off in second gear, and was driven from Bexhill to Glasgow using only third and fourth.

The car ran in the Scottish Trial, and then between London and Glasgow, stopping on Sundays, to complete 15,000 miles. It was then stripped and parts needed to make it perfect, for water-pump and steering, costing £2 2s 7d were fitted. The car weighed two tons but

(1) A high and handsome cabriolet on the 1911 Ghost chassis, showing rear quarters open to the elements. *(2) A later Ghost, a landaulette body on a 1916 chassis with tubular front bumper which suggests American origins, as do the headlamps. Note the small electric sidelamps and twin, side-mounted spare wheels. (3) An unusual limousine body by Lawton of Liverpool on a 1911 Ghost chassis with tulip back, front-mounted Stepney spare rim and six running lamps, including twin carriage lamps. The chauffeur is out in the weather again. (4) A wonderful example of the coachbuilder's art on the sought-after 1931 Phantom Two Continental. (5) The last year of the Silver Ghost, 1925, produced this Barker-bodied example of the touring car which looks much later. (6) A much earlier Ghost (1911) with the low bonnet line and screen folded down in the sporting manner.*

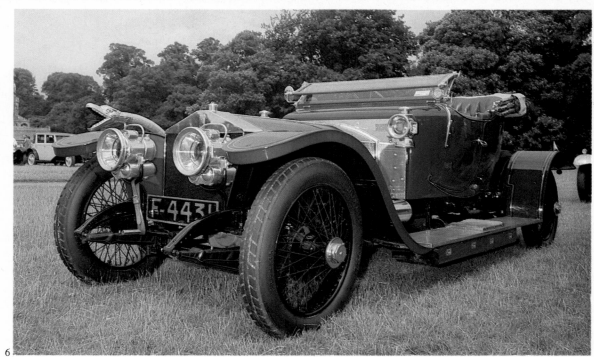

would run from 3 to 53 miles an hour in third and on to a top rate of 63 mph, and also do 17.8 miles to the gallon, at a cost per mile in those days of 4.5 pence.

The Ghost went into production in 1907 at the rate of four a week, and by 1926 a total of 8,416 Ghosts had been made, including American production from the Springfield factory opened in 1919. The power output of 48 bhp from seven litres is laughable today, and so is the compression ratio of 3.2:1, but it was produced at 1,250 rpm—tickover speed—the car doing 38 mph at 1,000 rpm. It could be driven at 5 mph at 300 rpm or so, justifying Royce's comment that the quality would still be appreciated long after the price had been forgotten.

Among the refinements on the Ghost was a governor which would keep the car at a constant speed up or down hill, without driver intervention, like a modern cruise control. Royce was as fussy as ever, and brake drums which started out as 106 lb castings weighed only 32 lb by the time they were machined and finished, whilst connecting rods

Ghost for use by Lawrence of Arabia's forces. Despite being twice the normal weight, these cars proved reliable.

The Ghost thus became the foundation-stone of Rolls-Royce's success.

—CHAPTER FOUR—

shed six pounds to come down from eight to two.

Another stunt run was from London to Edinburgh in 1911 in top gear only, in response to another Napier challenge. Later at the Brooklands track the Ghost did 78.26 mph and 34.32 mpg. It was not strictly a standard model, but with engine and suspension modifications plus a higher axle and single-seat racing body it did 101.8 mph. Some London to Edinburgh cars were sold as a special version.

A team of three cars built to the London-Edinburgh specification, together with a fourth privately entered, ran in the 1913 Austrian Alpine Trial with some success. This model became known as the Alpine Eagle.

During the first world-war, armoured bodies were fitted to the

In view of the great success of Rolls-Royce aero engines from before the second world war, when the Merlin was so vital, right up to date, it is a sad twist of fate that Charles Rolls should have died in an air crash before his company had entered that field of manufacture. He was, as we have seen, the first man to achieve a non-stop double crossing of the Channel, in June of 1910.

A month later, piloting his Wright Flyer, built under licence by Short Brothers in England with a modified tailplane of French design, at a meeting in Bournemouth, Rolls crashed on landing and died instantly.

Ironically, Rolls had wanted Royce to add a plane-making company

(1) An Auster rear screen keeps the wind off the rear-seat passengers in this 1918 example of the 40/50 Ghost, with touring body and cantilever rear springs. (2) The modern jury-rigged ignition coil on top of the engine spoils the under-bonnet looks of this 1912 Ghost, which also has twin carburettors, a non-standard feature. (3) This Yellow car wears a body said to have been designed by Barker but built by the Indian firm of Khan, on a 1913 Ghost chassis.

3

(4) Shown here is a 1913 Limousine on the 40/50 Ghost chassis, with the appropriate Standing Lady 'Spirit of Ecstasy' mascot designed by Charles Sykes, and many period features like carriage lamps, built-in roof rack and leather holder for the fixed starting-handle. (5) A typical Ghost tourer with open four-seat body and Stepney spare rim mounted on the driver's side running board.

4

5

to the car concern, but Henry Royce was never over-enthusiastic about aeroplanes.

Royce's caution extended to any modification or 'improvement' in the cars, and he was one of the last makers to adopt frontwheel brakes, as he believed that to steer and brake the same wheel must be wrong. Eventually he agreed to four-wheel brakes, but did not use them until 1925, when Royce looked at the systems of Hispano-Suiza and Renault in France and evolved a combination of the two, driven by a shaft from the gearbox to provide servo action or what we now call power assistance.

Royce still won his point, as the Rolls brakes were so arranged that if the rear wheel brakes locked the servo freed the front ones, thus retaining steering control. The Alpine Eagle model which had developed from the Alpine trial, had more than 150 modifications. Johnson did not like the name Eagle and called the car the Continental, which became the official designation.

Perhaps this objection arose from the incident in the 1912 Austrian Alpine Trial, when the private entrant James Radley, a friend of Rolls, stalled on the Katschberg Pass and could not get up. This led to modifications, including a new four-speed gearbox with a direct drive top instead of overdrive and a very low bottom gear. The tapered radiator as on the Edinburgh car also became standard in 1913, although lengthened, and cantilever rear springs were added.

Royce was 40 before he became involved in car construction, which may account for his conservatism. Although his American competitor Cadillac had an electric starter in 1913, Royce did not fit an electric starter and a dynamo for the lights until 1919, some Rolls owners having added their own before this, as can be seen from contemporary photographs of the cars.

The original Silver Ghost was sold in 1908 to a Mr Dan Hanbury, who covered more than 500,000 miles in it, before it was sold back again, in 1948, to the Rolls-Royce company in part exchange for another car.

(1) A sporting Ghost with a light skiff-type body in two-seater form, and no visible spare wheel, which must be mounted in the boat-tail. This is the 1912 twin-carburettor version of which the engine is shown in close-up on page 16, based on the Alpine Eagle or Continental model. (2) A 1914 Ghost 40/50, described as a Colonial model, with Auster rear screen, rear luggage rack and both handbrake and gear-change lever mounted outside the bodywork, together with the Klaxon horn. This example has cantilever springs which were fitted from 1912-25, and carries a complete spare wheel and tyre, not just a tyre mounted on a detachable rim.

(1) The American Silver Ghost can be identified by the wheels (indented wheel nuts), bumpers, lamps, side-wings to windscreen and Twenty-type horizontal shutters on radiator. White sidewalled tyres are usually American too. This car was made at the Springfield factory in 1922 and had a Smith-Springfield body. Manufacture in Spingfield began in the winter of 1919, and the company went into liquidation in 1936, although manufacture had ceased long before this. The company had earlier bought up Brewster, who built most of the American bodies. There were many problems in making the Rolls-Royce in the United States, and the venture was not a success. (4) Another American-

3

built car on which all the features can be spotted: indented wheel nuts, white sidewalls, cylindrical lamps, tubular bumpers, and rather strange body-lines. The American cars used Bosch magnetos, Delco coil ignition from General Motors, Bijur generators, and were lefthand drive only from 1925. The three-speed box was controlled by a central gear-lever. A total of 1,703 Silver Ghosts were made at Springfield, Massachussetts from 1921-26. Before 1925, American cars, like the British, used dual coil and magneto ignition. The later British-built cars had a four-speed gearbox with direct top, after a period of three-speed gearbox use.

4

The 30 horsepower six-cylinder model of 1906 was exhibited at the Paris Salon and in New York. However, only 37 examples were ever made, of which just one remains. (2) A 1910 Silver Ghost with open touring body by Barker. (3) A 1912 Hooper Limousine on the Silver Ghost chassis, with high top-hamper carrying the spare wheel. (4) The picture shows the induction side of a 1912 Silver Ghost engine, with its single up-draught carburettor. (5) An Alpine Eagle version of the Silver Ghost, with light sporting touring body. Officially known as the Continental, these cars were a much modified chassis development of the models run in the Alpine trials. (6) The engine of a 1924 Ghost, showing inlet manifold mounted above the exhaust. The ancillaries, (dynamo and magneto) can be seen lower down close to the frame.

1

2

from one hole to another changed over the ignition from coil to magneto. In addition to making driving easier by providing a constant cruising speed, the governor also made gear-changing easier if one used the technique taught in the Rolls-Royce school.

Royce did not trust springs to hold his gear selectors in place. On the Tourist Trophy car the driver had to make a change from second to third in five motions: left, to clear the notch; forward, to reach the gate; right, to cross the gate; back to engage third; and then left, to align with the notch. Fortunately, most running on the early Rolls cars can be done in top gear, or at worst in third.

3

4

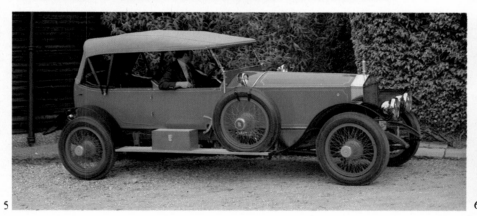

5

6

One of the instances of Royce's genius is that he anticipated the problem of vibration in six-cylinder crankshafts, now universally known as the 'skipping rope' effect, in his 40/50 engine of 1906.

He used seven main bearings and made his connecting rods from nickel steel forgings machined all over to reveal any flaws in the metal. The gears driving the camshaft were honed by hand for 80 hours to make them perfectly silent. The cylinder heads were in one with the blocks and not detachable, but had caps over the valves. A trained chauffeur could change a valve in four minutes, the spare valve of course carried on the car in a fitted wooden case. Rolls-Royce run a school to train their drivers, who are awarded a diploma on satisfactory completion of the course.

Chassis were bolted together with tapered bolts, each one worked to fit its own hole, with square heads. The 40/50 had two batteries, one a spare for emergency use, and two ignition systems; one coil and one magneto. This was continued in later cars, when simply switching a lead

Royce would have nothing to do with chains, then, as now, used by many designers to drive camshafts for instance. He had gears, and a shaft to his rear axle, not side chains as on many cars of the period. Royce's father had died when he was nine years old, which made his early life hard, and he learnt much of his engineering skill in the backyard shed of a Mr Yarrow, with whom he lodged when a railway apprentice, where various machines were housed.

It was in the railway workshops that Royce learned that there was only one correct way to do a job; time was no object, but the task had to be properly done. He learned engineering principles, the use of different metals both hot and cold, and the need for accurate fitting and machining. He never budged from these principles in the making of his motor-cars, nor would he allow anyone else to do so.

Royce started in business by selling an electric bell for use in people's homes for 18 pence and went on through bigger electrical projects until he was making big cranes for the docks. When he married Minnie Punt

(1, 2) The bright-yellow coachwork on this 1923 Twenty chassis matched the horse-racing colours of its owner Lord Lonsdale. (3) A typical 1930s drophead coupé four-seater with disc wheels, outside hood-irons, front quarter-lights, trumpet horns, running boards and harmonic bumpers. Dare one say it has a typical Mark V Jaguar look, although that car came later? This has the lines of a Mulliner body, as used on Phantom II and other models.

he took a house at Knutsford near Manchester with a large garden and became a gardening enthusiast, but he spent so much time at the factory that he did his digging and planting at night with the aid of a light bulb on a stick stuck in the ground. His partner, A.E. Claremont, married his wife's sister.

Royce became so absorbed in his work that he did not eat, which led to his breakdown, and his accountant, Mr De Looze would send boys around the works carrying glasses of milk, with orders not to return until Royce had drunk it. Claremont the accountant never trusted Royce's cars, although he had to use one, so he had a horse-cab follow him, and a plate on the car's dash read: 'If the car breaks down don't ask a lot of silly questions.'

—CHAPTER FIVE—

After the first world war there was a depression in car sales, and Royce, deciding that a smaller car was needed, designed the Baby Rolls, or Twenty. He began work in 1919 on a 3.5 litre car which eventually emerged in 1922 as the first Rolls-Royce with overhead valves, and is distinguishable from the front by its horizontal radiator shutters.

The Twenty ran for eight years up to 1929 and a total of 2,940 were made at Derby. The car was a six-cylinder with the same stroke as the original Silver Ghost but of course a smaller 76 mm bore, whereas the Ghost had had square dimensions of 114×114 mm. It was just under 15 feet long and the chassis weighed 2,542 lb. Surprisingly, a three-speed gearbox in unit with the engine with a central gear lever was used, whereas all previous Rolls-Royce models had placed the gear-lever and handbrake on the driver's right, giving rise to the joke that one needed to wear plus fours or breeches to get in and out of the car.

In 1925 the company substituted a four-speed gearbox and moved the operating lever back to the driver's right. Rolls owners were conservative and did not like too many changes. The Earl of Londsdale, for instance, found he could not wear his top hat in his Twenty, so he had

the body from his 1910 Daimler mounted onto his 1923 Twenty to make room for his headgear.

Another change in the Twenty was that it had coil ignition only, and Royce himself explained in an article in *The Autocar* that this was quite satisfactory, his aim being simplicity, 'but not at the expense of perfection'. The Twenty was powered by an engine of 3,150 c.c. and cost £1,590 as an open tourer, although many more saloons were sold, some of them much too heavy for the power available, which traditionally was never revealed beyond saying it was 'adequate'.

(4) An early 'doctor's coupé' with Brookes rear trunk on outside luggage grid. It is a 1925 Twenty with Barker body. (5) A rebodied 1926 Twenty with a later Compton body in the 'thirties manner. The headlamps give away the car's age. (6) Engine layout of the 20/25 and 25/30, with big overhead air cleaner, dual ignition and single carburettor. Overleaf: An aluminium torpedo touring body by Barker, on a Phantom I chassis, was made for the Nawab Wali-ud Dowla Bahadur of Hyderabad.

Body space was claimed to be ample for six seats, special care having been taken to ensure low rear seating. The car also featured detachable cylinder head and a monobloc cylinder casting instead of the previous group of two. Aluminium pistons were now used, and engine fumes were drawn back into the induction system to keep them away from passengers.

The famous horizontal radiator shutters were controlled by the driver, aided by a gauge on the dash, to keep the engine running at the right temperature. When the four-speed gearbox model appeared in 1925/6, *The Autocar* commented that it was 'a very considerable improvement'. By now the car had the benefit of four-wheel brakes for the first time, using the French-based servo system.

Royce began designing the Twenty at a time when the company had 300 unsold Silver Ghosts in stock due to the recession, and his brief was to build a car of the same quality as the big one, to sell for about £1,500. The Ghost was then a 15-year-old design, but Royce had much

earlier bought the twin overhead camshaft Peugeot which had won the 1912 French Grand Prix. He had already patented an ohc design in 1910, and now produced two prototypes, the Goshawk I with overhead cams and the Goshawk II with pushrods, as it eventually emerged.

Rolls offered their Twenty chassis with two different steering column angles, one upright for chauffeur-driven limousines and the other raked for sporting owner-driver bodies. A standard open tourer complete with body was offered for £1,590, close to Royce's original brief of £1,500.

The Twenties were tested over 10,000 miles on rough French roads at the new company depot at Chateauroux, 150 miles south of Paris. In spite of some breakdowns, the car proved to be the quiet, reliable vehicle that the buyers wanted.

Rolls-Royce, in the person of Claude Johnson, had been taking an

have better fittings.' There were however differences with the local management and costs rose to exceed forecasts.

By 1921 only five cars a week were being made instead of the promised 12. It was found that Americans would not buy a chassis and wait for a body to be built, in the English way, so some stock bodies were offered from various coachbuilders. Problems were mounting, and Johnson who had masterminded the American operation, died in 1926.

The American recession of 1929 did not help, and the American company filed its bankruptcy petition in 1935. The name had earlier been changed to the Springfield Manufacturing Corporation, to avoid associating Rolls-Royce with the failure. It was a sad end to a brave experiment, with a total production of 1,703 American Silver Ghosts. The Twenty was not considered suitable for the American market and was not made there, nor was the Phantom I which followed the Ghost.

—CHAPTER SIX—

interest in the American car market ever since the 1906 Tourist Trophy race victory, however it was not until November 1919 that an American Rolls-Royce company was formed as Rolls-Royce of America Inc. The capital was raised locally but the company run from England.

Rolls-Royce took over the Wire Wheel Works in Springfield, Massachusetts, and were making engines by July 1920 under the supervision of British foremen. Experts reported that American electrical equipment was superior to British, and recommended using it for all RR cars, but there were problems because of differences in petrol, and climate. The cheaper American-made chassis were also said to be better made than the imported ones.

Most of the bodies were built by Brewster on Long Island, and an inspector reported: 'The best American bodies are better built and finished than the English. They are made to more practical designs and

By 1924 Rolls-Royce were experiencing a fall-off in sales of the Twenty. A new model was required to replace the 17 year old Silver Ghost, as well as to counter the competition from other manufacturers. In May 1925 the New Phantom was announced, now generally known as the Phantom I.

Despite being heavier and taller, the Phantom was faster than the Ghost. It was powered by a 7,668 c.c. overhead valve six-cylinder engine with detachable head, in long and short-chassis versions, and in all 2,212 were made, plus 1,241 lefthand drive American models made at Springfield. Although it had two cylinder blocks of three, they were covered by a single cast-iron head. The engine was like a big version of the Twenty, with some differences. Later versions had an aluminium cylinder head in place of the cast-iron one, which could cause 'pinking'

A 1923 Barker-bodied tourer on the Twenty chassis with splendid bulb-horn on the offside running board. (2) A Twenty four-seat tourer with rear Auster screen, a metal rear half-tonneau and a period accessory; a tyre-mounted rearview mirror. (3) A 1914 Silver Ghost with four-seat tourer body and low sporting windscreen. The built-out wire wheels and herringbone-pattern tyres give a more authentic air. The absence of a driver's door, was a common omission, with the spare wheel, brake and gear lever all in the way on the driver's righthand side.

and had a top speed of 64 mph in the highest ratio of the four-speed gearbox. A total of 2,212 Phantoms were built between 1925 and 1929. (3) Shown here is another sedanca, this one based on a 1934 Phantom II chassis. The Phantom II was made from 1929-35, a total of 1,767 examples having been produced. (4) A Thrupp & Maberly sedanca body on a Phantom II chassis, with fancy individual running-boards or steps. (5) An interesting Anglo-American Phantom II model, with body originally built by Park Ward in 1929, but rebodied by Brewster, the American coachbuilder, around 1932. (6) A more sporting skiff-type body on a Phantom. Overleaf: A magnificent American-made Phantom cabriolet.

(1, 2) An imposing example of the Phantom I in sedanca form with open chauffeur compartment and enclosed passenger area. The driver's section has a retracting roof which recedes into the space between the roof and headlining of the rear compartment. The Phantom I had the advantage over its predecessor, the Silver Ghost, of having brakes on the front wheels, as can be seen in the illustration. A mechanical servo system was used to assist these drum brakes. The six-cylinder engine was made in two blocks of three, with a one-piece detachable head. Overhead valves now replaced the side-valves used on the Ghost. The car weighed nearly 6,000 lbs.

and running-on due to overheating. It had two plugs per cylinder, one fed by coil and the other by magneto.

The chassis of the new car was almost identical to the Ghost, and the short models tended to be open tourers or owner-driver saloons, with formal coachwork on the long cars. The new overhead valve engine was supposed to give a better performance than the old side-valve Ghost, but this depended largely on the weight of the bodywork.

The Phantom I was to last only 5 years before being updated into the Phantom II, to counter Bentley's entry into the fast saloon market, as well as the fierce competition from makers such as Cadillac, Duesenberg, Hispano-Suiza, Isotta-Fraschini and Pierce-Arrow.

Bentley themselves were now in serious financial trouble when the diamond millionaire Woolf Barnato withdrew his support. Rolls heard that Napier, whose 6.5 and 8 litre 100 mph cars were already a serious threat, intended to buy the Bentley concern. The successful Rolls bid was made under the British Central Equitable Trust name, and in the ensuing deal, the services of W.O. Bentley were acquired, thus preventing him from designing cars for competitors.

The Phantom II produced more power from its engine than the New Phantom, and although RR did not publish the figures, the new

car probably had 120 bhp compared with 100 from its predecessor. This may not be a lot from 7.7 litres but all Royce engines were very unstressed. The PII also used a hyphoid rear axle and no torque tube from gearboxes to axle, which allowed a low floor-line in the limousine bodies which were bound to be fitted.

Coachbuilders were helped by a sub-frame, enabling bodies to be built at the same time as the chassis, thus speeding-up total production. By now many coachbuilders were making bodies for RR frames, the old Barker monopoly no longer existed. The PII also had one-shot chassis lubrication which lubricated all grease points, except those on the axles, at the press of a plunger. Later this was extended to a complete lubrication system for the whole chassis.

1

2

3

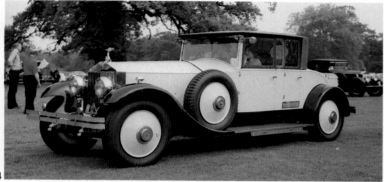

4

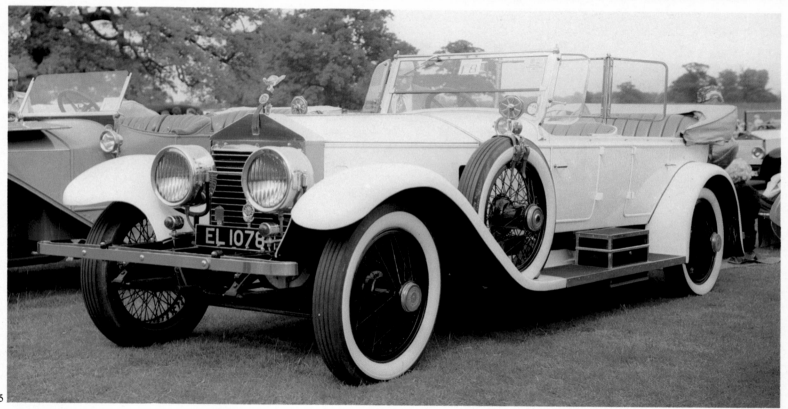

5

(1) A 1928 Phantom I taking part in an English RR rally in 1975, with formal D-back saloon bodywork. (2) A Barker-bodied barrel-sided tourer in polished aluminium, unpainted, also on the rally field. (3) A superb Silver Ghost limousine of 1911. (4) A Phantom I with a curious three-door coupé body. (5) A Silver Ghost tourer with rear Auster screen, sidewings to the windscreen and white sidewall tyres, which suggest an American origin. (6) A pretty Phantom I with open tourer body, three-piece windscreen and outside Klaxon.

6

(1) This 1930 Thrupp & Maberly
sports cabriolet de ville PII won the 1978
Concours d'Elegance *of the Rolls-*
Royce Enthusiasts Club. *(2) A 1938*
Wraith four-door four-light saloon in
sober colouring with projecting boot and
disc wheels. (3) A ravishing 1933
Phantom II Continental faux-cabriolet,
with white sidewall tyres and twin
rear-mounted spare wheels, taking part in
a concours in England. This car has
exceptional elegance of line and beautiful
proportions which disguise its great size.
An outstanding design.

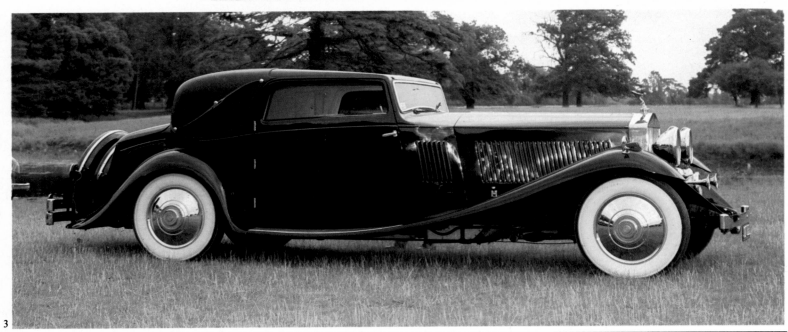

4

5

The Phantom II made its debut at the 1929 Olympia show in London, at a price of £2,935 for a Barker saloon, £2,960 for a Hooper limousine, or chassis only at £1,900. This was hardly cheap in terms of money value then, but there were two more expensive competitors on show: the Duesenberg at £2,380 for the chassis and the sporting Mercedes-Benz 38/250 at a chassis price of £2,150, both of them after paying 30 per cent import duty.

It was too difficult to manufacture the Phantom II at Springfield with all the engineering changes, so a lefthand driver version was built at Derby, and exported to Europe as well. Many beautiful bodies were built upon the new Rolls chassis, but the model now most sought after by enthusiasts is the Phantom II short-chassis Continental, originally built to the special order of Henry Royce for his own use, although it does not appear that he ever drove it.

The Continental body was based on the Riley Nine Monaco saloon. Rolls had an example of this close-coupled machine taken apart at his house, and after careful measurement, the Phantom II chassis was altered so that rear passengers could be moved forward and given foot

(4) The Belgian coachbuilder
Vanden Plas, best known for his Bentley bodies, built this foursome drophead coupé on a 25/30 RR chassis. (5) Car nearest camera is a 1938 Hooper-bodied Phantom III with formal four-door, four-light saloon coachwork, powered by the V12 cylinder 7338 cc engine derived from the company's aircraft designs.

Shown alongside is an earlier Phantom. (6) Sedanca-de-ville body on 1927 Phantom I with front portion open. The one-piece windscreen gives the car a modern air.

6

(1) Rolls-Royce wheel-hub controls, beautifully and precisely made, operate the ignition (Late and Early for the spark) and Throttle (Open and Closed) via the two levers. There is also a mixture control. In the centre of the boss is the horn button, and on many models there is another control elsewhere for Town and Country loudness of the horns. *(2) A*

space with deep foot-wells. The Continental appeared with stronger rear springs, higher axle-ratio, low rake steering column and a ride control adjustable from the driving seat.

Moving the rear-seat passengers forward altered the weight distribution on the Continental, but Royce solved this—as he had on the Twenty—by moving the spare wheels (two in this case) from the side-mounts in the front wings to the rear of the car, thus adding to the sporting appearance. The Continental would do a little over 90 miles an

very handsome Phantom II foursome drophead coupé bodied by H. J. Mulliner, with wheel discs. *(3) A 1913 Ghost with cantilever springs and a rather bilious finish. (4) A Springfield Phantom with Brewster body and American bumpers, white sidewalls, Brookes rear trunk, American lamps, folding head, and cantilever springs. (5) A rebodied 1926 Twenty which was fitted with this foursome drophead coupé at a later date in the 'thirties style. This car is a good-looking one, but it cannot have had sparkling performance with all that weight behind the little Twenty engine.*

4

5

ROLLS AND BENTLEY

(1, 2) Bentley, who were to be bought-out by Rolls-Royce on their collapse in 1933, made this magnificent 6.5 litre sports car in 1930 and then ran out of money. Rolls-Royce feared these cars as competitors and bought up the company to keep it out of Napier's hands. Rolls-Royce acquired the services of the founder and designer, Walter Owen Bentley, together with the assets, but he was never allowed to design a car for them. The cars are introduced as relevant to RR history, as the later so-called Rolls-Bentley ('the silent sports car') developed from this situation, although they were entirely different from what is now called the Vintage Bentley as opposed to the Derby Bentley built by Rolls. (3, 4 and 5) show the three-litre Bentley Speed model from the same stable.

hour and reach 60 mph from rest in just under 20 seconds.

It is difficult for us now to appreciate the qualities of cars like the Continental, which seem rough in comparison with the designs of 50 years later, but in its day it was a superlative machine in terms of ride, performance, and smoothness. Even so, it was outpaced by some of its rivals, which led to the introduction of the even more advanced Phantom III, dealt with in the next chapter.

—CHAPTER SEVEN—

Rolls-Royce produced their first Bentley car, after taking over the old Bentley company, in 1933—the year of Sir Henry Royce's death. It was built at Derby and inevitably became known as the Rolls-Bentley, to distinguish it from the Rolls-Royce and the Cricklewood Bentley, although this was never an official name. His company in Manchester continued making electrical equipment up to about the time of his death aged 70, on April 22.

The 3.5 litre Rolls-Bentley and the later 4.25 litre models, developments of the Rolls-Royce 20/25 and the 25/30 respectively, will be considered in the next chapter. They were developed by W. O. Bentley, now employed by Rolls-Royce, and used twin carburettors and other modifications to give a more sporting image.

In the year of Royce's death, the colour of the enamel filling in the

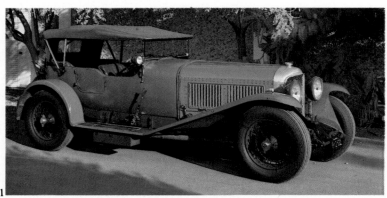

1

2

3

4

5

(4) A special-bodied Bentley from the Rolls-Bentley period (1933) which had its 3.5 litre engine up-rated to 4.5 litres, like the car run by Eddie Hall in the T.T. He did well for a private owner without official factory backing. (5) An imposing frontal view of a Phantom with twin side-mounts in metal holders and full complement of horns and lamps on the front apron. Note the wheel-mounted mirrors on either side. (6) A frontal view of the American Phantom III, with what looks from its lines like a Park Ward body very similar to that on the English car alongside in picture (5).

(1) The R-Type Continental Bentley of 1952 is much treasured by enthusiasts of the marque, and a modern classic which will keep its value. It was powered by a six-cylinder in-line engine and fitted with either manual or automatic transmission. (2) A Rolls-Royce Phantom III of 1938 with Hooper body on formal lines, designed as a limousine with division between front and rear. The rear-hinged doors would not be acceptable by today's safety standards, but they were convenient. (3) An American-registered Phantom III of 1936 with unusual rear wheel spats in a four-door, four-light body with shallow windscreen and white sidewall tyres. It has clean, uncluttered lines which make it look imposing and smaller than it really is.

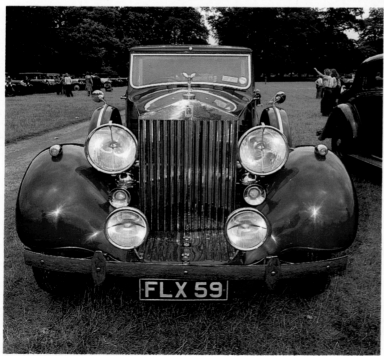

lettering on the radiator badge was changed from red to black, as we have already seen. The story went round and is still current, that this was in mourning for one of the company's founders and its chief guiding spirit, but the truth is more mundane. Royce had decided, before his final illness, that red clashed with certain body colours, and as he wanted everything not only to be perfect but to be seen to be so, this had to be changed.

Like many others, this legend about the car and its makers persists. The story often recounted is of an axle failure which was rectified, but apparently no bill arrived for the work. On enquiry the customer was informed that no record of an axle breakdown existed. Stories such as this can seldom be substantiated. A friend of mine once stopped in Spain to help a Rolls-Royce owner in trouble with his automatic transmission. He just happened to be passing and an automatic transmission expert by trade, unconnected with Rolls-Royce, but the owner will for ever believe that he was sent by a combination of the company and divine providence.

Soon after Royce's death the company, needing an even more powerful and up-to-date car to stay in contention with the other esoteric marques, produced their biggest and most sophisticated car to date; the Phantom III with a V12 light alloy engine.

The Phantom III came on the market in 1936, and was a complete departure from its predecessors, with a separate pressed steel chassis frame, a V12 engine derived from Rolls' very successful aero engines which had powered fighters and bombers, and independent front suspension from an American General Motors design, modified as always to suit Rolls standards and requirements.

The company had considered a V8 or straight 8 engine, and had experimented for years, as always, before adopting any new piece of

(1) The Phantom VI is the largest of the current Rolls-Royce models, and is powered by the 6750 cc V8 engine that was originally developed for the Silver Shadow II. (2) Another individual sedanca-de-ville body on a 1931 20/25 chassis with individual step boards and side-mounted spare wheel. (3) The view from the front of a 1930s drophead coupé with four-seat body and the usual display of horns and driving lamps, plus pillar-mounted headlamps.

2

equipment, but they did not find the degree of smoothness satisfactory. The V12 used hydraulic tappets as on some American makes, hitherto unknown in England. Now that the cars are old this is the first feature which enthusiasts remove and convert to normal solid operation. They may have worked better when new.

The Phantom III would do more than 90 mph although it weighed anything up to 6,000 lb, the chassis alone being more than 4,000 lb. It was propelled by 7.340 litres at a fuel consumption of around ten miles to the gallon. It cost £2,500 with the cheapest body, up to £3,000 with some others, and was 17 feet long. It was produced until the start of World War Two in 1939, with detail improvements, and although so many of them had sporting lines there was considerable passenger space. A total of 717 were made with all kinds of different bodywork.

The Phantom III was the greatest of the pre-war machines, and

conceived in Royce's time although he did not live to see it. He had been made a baronet in 1930 after the victory of British aeroplanes with Rolls-Royce engines in the Schneider Trophy air race in 1929, a feat repeated in 1931. Royce returned to England to die after spending the winter in France at his villa in the sun.

Work on the Phantom III had in fact begun a year before Royce's death in April 1933, when his engineers visited the United States and found that the big-car makers were using vee engines with 12 and even 16 cylinders, and General Motors had introduced independent front suspension, which Rolls-Royce eventually used under licence. The code-name, the company always used one, for the Phantom III when under development was Spectre, in keeping with the Ghosts and Phantoms and foreshadowing the Shadows, Wraiths, and Spirits.

The Phantom III did not re-emerge after the 1939-45 war as it would

THE BLACK BADGE

(1, 2, 3) The famous 'Blower Bentley' which for all its reputation never won a race. This model was developed in the dying days of the old Bentley company from the standard four-cylinder 4½ litre model for Dorothy Paget and Sir Henry Birkin, with design by Amherst Villiers, who provided the supercharger on the nose of the crank. The tops of the two SU carburettors can be seen behind the apron on the right in the top picture.

W. O. Bentley himself was always opposed to supercharging, which he said was a perversion of design. He preferred to make the engine bigger. A special heavy crank had to be developed for the Blower Bentley, and its critics said the engine was not up to rotating this heavy mass of metal, but it remains a legend despite its lack of success in competition and is considered the epitome of the Bulldog Drummond era of brutish arrogance. (4, 6) Another great classic, the 12-cylinder vee-engined Phantom III Rolls-Royce of 1937, which owed much to the company's successful aero-engines used in fighters and bombers. It was produced to compete with Hispano-Suiza, Isotta Fraschini, Cadillac, and

others who were producing massive engines of eight cylinders or so with big power outputs, so Rolls designed the finest car of them all with a V12 engine. The vee was at 60 degrees and the block of light alloy with cast-iron wet liners, alloy detachable cylinder heads, overhead valves and a single camshaft. American style hydraulic tappets were used up to 1938, but these proved to be unreliable. It had a seven-bearing crankshaft, dual ignition and two plugs per cylinder, so that finding a misfire was a nightmare. There was a four-speed synchromesh gearbox and 90 mph performance in a car weighing two-and-a-half tons. (5) The Rolls-built Bentley supercar ('the silent sports car') of 1939 MX type 4.25 litre overdrive model. This was developed when Bentley owners, driving on the new Autobahnen in Germany at consistently high cruising speeds, ran their big-end bearings, and the overdrive, by reducing the revolutions, was thought to be the answer. It was in fact a geared-up top, not an added overdrive.

1

3

have been impossibly expensive to produce. Like most models of the time it was first seen at the Olympia show in 1935 and was arguably the most advanced car then being made anywhere, and probably the best-made as well. The wheelbase was actually 2 inches less than the short version of the PII, but in chassis form weighed 240 lb more.

It cost only £50 more than the much less sophisticated earlier car, according of course to coachwork. Sadly Barkers, who had been in existence since the 18th century, went out of business in 1938 and made some of their last bodies on the PIII, one of them a beautiful close-coupled sports saloon that would have gladdened the heart of Sir Henry Royce.

The Phantom III was hardly suitable for the DIY owner to work on in the unlikely event that he should want to. It was incredibly complicated and components were hard to get at, including the clutch, sparking plugs, and so on. Rolls-Royce did not make much money out of these cars, but we shall not see their like again.

—CHAPTER EIGHT—

About the same time (1929) as the Phantom II was replacing the Phantom I, another new Rolls-Royce model appeared, the 20/25, which lasted until 1936. It was a development of the Twenty, powered by a 3,669 c.c. six-cylinder engine with the customary Rolls righthand change lever for the four-speed box. A total of 3,827 were made, and the model was readily distinguishable from the Twenty by the vertical radiator shutters instead of the horizontal ones used on the earlier car.

The new model had an enlarged engine with a higher compression ratio and a new crankshaft, and could be run up to 4,000 revolutions a minute instead of only the lower limit of the older car. This was in fact a factory test figure, but owners were permitted to use 3,500 rpm on the road, ludicrously low by today's standards but not at that time, bearing in mind the limited understanding of metallurgy and dynamics. In any event, Rolls-Royces were always made to be driven in a high gear with the engine turning as slowly as possible. Bottom-gear torque, or good

4

5

6

(1) A 1939 Wraith, made in the year that RR bought Park Ward, who built this four-door, four-light saloon. Only 491 Wraiths were made. (2) Head-on view of a 20/25 sports saloon with division and a Barker body. The 20/25 was a development of the Twenty, made from 1929-36 with better engine and brakes. (3) A rather uninspired four-door six-light saloon with D-back on the 20/25 chassis in chocolate and cream finish. (4) A pretty 20/25 cabriolet by Offord, built in 1936.

pulling power at low speed, was one of the characteristics which Royce always demanded.

In 1932 some of the Phantom characteristics were applied to the 20/25, including a steeper rake to the steering column, a large thin-rim steering wheel, a lower and wider radiator cap, flatter front springs, grouped instruments, and grouped lubrication points. The performance was also improved without sacrificing the traditional qualities of enduring silence, docility, and extreme controllability.

Other changes included a larger radiator, a modified exhaust system, double-acting hydraulic shock absorbers front and rear, and alternative ignition systems. The normal running system was coil ignition, but there was a magneto permanently installed ready for use, to which the driver could switch by moving a lead from one connector to another. This was not quite as simple as on the Phantom, on which it could be done from the driving seat, but did provide an insurance against breakdown where no ignition spares were available.

The radiator shutters were thermostatically controlled so that the driver no longer had to watch his temperature gauge and make adjustments himself. The small Rolls-Royce, as this model was known, 5

(5) The world's ugliest car? A 1934 four-door saloon with projecting boot on the 20/25 produced by Connaught. The 20/25 was the best-selling Royce between the two World Wars, but there were prettier bodies than this. (6, 7 and 8)

6

Pictures show different views of another odd body on a 20/25 chassis, this time a sedanca-de-ville by the French firm of Fernandez and Darrin. The car was shown at the 1935 Paris salon and bought by Lady Davis of Montreal. It looks rather like the halves of two different cars joined together.

7

8

was now established and a good seller alongside its big brother.

In 1936 the 20/25 engine was enlarged by increasing the bore to 4,257 c.c., becoming the 25/30. It was better known as the 4¼ Bentley, which was the same car but with a more sporting character. The chassis of the 25 was a strengthened version of the 20/25, the wheelbase was three inches longer and the track slightly wider. It was at around this time that Rolls put their trust in specialist component manufacturers and began buying-in various parts instead of manufacturing everything themselves. This included steering gear and the built-in jacks fitted to some models.

In all 1,201 examples of the 25 were sold between 1936 and 1938, and it became the final development of the Twenty, before the introduction of a completely new car.

The new car was the Wraith. It abandoned the system of tapered bolts made to fit one special hole in the chassis and substituted welding, which was perhaps stiffer and better but was not in the Rolls-Royce tradition. There was also a new six-cylinder light alloy engine, and the car was both longer and wider.

One long-overdue change in the engine was to separate the inlet

THE MEDIUM SIZED ROLLS

(1) Barker built most of the early RR bodies, including this beautiful 1910 Torpedo Tourer on a Silver Ghost chassis. It has many special features, and the lamps and fittings are silver-plated, although the car is painted white. (2) An equally lovely Phantom III close-coupled sports coupé with four-door bodywork and encased side-mounted spare wheel with clean, uncluttered lines. PIIIs tended to have shallow, slot-like windscreens which do not support today's safety standards, but they helped give a low roofline.

2

and exhaust ports, which had both been on the same side, and put them one set either side, thus improving the breathing and producing more power. Some of the advantage of the extra power was lost as the car was heavier, but it was keen in price, being offered at £1,695 complete with a Park Ward four-door saloon body. Park Ward had by then been bought by Rolls-Royce and had replaced Barker as their body supplier, although other coachbuilders still existed.

The basic technique of construction came from the horsedrawn coaches they had built before the motorcar. The frame of the body was made in the same way, usually in ash, a hard wood, but the difference was that for cars they began making the panels out of aluminium or later steel, instead of the woods used in the horse era.

Most of the expensive cars in the early days of motoring were sold in chassis form, bodies being supplied by independent manufacturers. Car makers did however maintain an interest to avoid heavy, unsafe or ugly designs, and would often recommend coachmakers to the customer. Rolls-Royce used Mulliner, Park Ward and Thrupp & Maberly amongst others.

One of the problems associated with the admittedly crude way of making bodies with an ash frame with pieces of aluminium bent and nailed on, however beautiful they might look, was that they creaked and groaned at the woodwork joints, really designed for stationary objects like furniture. A way round this was invented by a M. Weymann in France, who kept the wooden components of the frame apart and linked

them with metal plates allowing the pieces to move independently. The resulting frame was covered with leather cloth, which looked dull but made a light and silent body.

Unfortunately spurious copies were made of the Weymann body which rapidly fell apart and gave the system a bad name. The next move was to press the panels for bodies on giant presses and weld them

(3) Another handsome car, the Silver Dawn, which was the Rolls version of the standard steel Mark VI Bentley, originally made only for export to the USA. This is a 1953 example. Between 1949 and 1955 only 760 were built. (4) A Hooper-bodied Silver Wraith of 1949 vintage. In all 1,700 were made from 1947 to 1959, all in chassis form with outside-built bodies. The Silver Wraith was the first postwar car and a new design, using independent front suspension and inlet-over-exhaust engine layout in a 4887 cc unit. (5) Another Silver Wraith of 1949, again in a two-tone finish which was the fashion of the day. Note the different lines of the rear window.

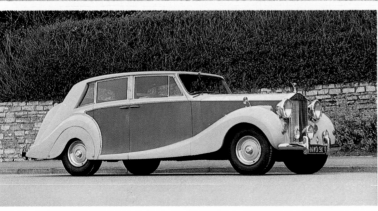

together, which produced a stronger and more durable result but meant that all cars made that way had to be alike, thus dispensing with coachbuilders, who gradually disappeared. Rolls-Royce continued with the coachbuilt body until the second world war, but when they resumed car production in 1946 it was with a pressed and welded body like everyone else.

Press-joined bodies make for longer model runs, as changing the tools and dies is expensive, and Rolls make so few cars, relatively speaking, that they must use the dies for a long time. They also impose such stringent tests on every part, that it takes a long time to have a complete new model approved in every particular and released for production.

POST-WAR CHANGES

The last pre-war model, the Wraith, lasted only two model years, 1938-39, and only 491 examples were made. After the war the first model on the market was the Silver Wraith which had a longer run, from 1947-59, with a sale of 1,783 examples. It had independent front suspension, hydraulic front brakes, pressed steel wheels, an optional automatic gearbox from 1952 and optional power steering assistance from 1956.

The Silver Wraith stayed with RR tradition in being available as a chassis only, with coachbuilt bodies from another supplier, but broke with tradition in many other ways. It had a 4,257 c.c. engine with overhead inlet valves and side exhaust, which had been in development since 1935. Dual ignition was dispensed with, and so were the gear-driven auxiliaries, and it became the first Rolls-Royce with a belt drive for the water pump, fan and dynamo.

For the first time the company revealed power output; in the car as opposed to on the test bed it was 122 bhp. It was to be the last RR offered without a pressed-steel body, as the coachbuilders, who had been making 1,500 bodies a year for Rolls and Bentley customers before the war, had largely gone out of business. The company now spent £250,000 on a set of press tools to have their own bodies made like any other car.

The first pressed-steel body car from the company was not a Rolls but the Bentley Mark VI. An identical Rolls called the Silver Dawn followed in 1949, and 761 were sold by the time it was discontinued in 1955. Originally it was for export to the U.S. only, and was not offered in Britain until 1953. One of the big and lasting changes was the

The making of a Rolls-Royce at the factory at Crewe, where care is all. (1) Lowering the body onto the mechanical components and sub-frames as final assembly begins. Special care is taken to spread the stress evenly. (2) Final balancing of the V8 engine is a delicate process carried out with the most modern machine aids. (3) Selecting veneers with matching grain for dashboard covering, which must give a mirror image from one side to the other. Many kinds of tree disappear into the interior of a Rolls-Royce. (4) The automatic gearbox, of American design, is bolted up to the Rolls-made V8 engine as the mechanical parts take shape. (5) Hand soldering is used in the famous Grecian radiator.

1

2

3

4

5

adoption of the General Motors Hydramatic transmission as used by Oldsmobile, although Rolls made it themselves under licence to incorporate their old gearbox-driven brake servo system. This transmission had four speeds when most automatics had either two or three.

The cars were now being made at Crewe instead of Derby, and in 1955 another step forward into the modern era of the RR came with the adoption of automatic transmission as standard on the next model, the Silver Cloud, which ran until 1962 in three models, the Silver Cloud I, II, and III, to a total of 5,075 units. The Cloud II in 1959 saw the adoption of a V8 engine in place of the in-line six, which had been standard since 1907.

The Cloud I came in two lengths, to provide for a saloon and a limousine, and at £4,669 was only £46 dearer than the much smaller and simpler Dawn. Mulliner, later bought by Rolls, offered a drophead

(1) The 1982 Rolls-Royce Silver Spur is a long wheel-base version of the Silver Spirit. It has more room in the rear compartment, a smaller rear window, Everflex roof covering and a distinctive trim. (2) The Silver Spirit is the standard Rolls-Royce saloon car. It is fitted with automatic air-conditioning and automatic gearbox as standard. The 6750 cc V8 engine is run for the equivalent of 50 miles on natural gas on the test bed while a tester keeps a check on it through a stethoscope. Twelve coats of paint are applied for the perfect body finish. (3) The Phantom VI is the world's most exclusive and expensive motor-car, the body being hand-built by Mulliner Park Ward. This seven seater is 19 ft. 10 in. long and includes a television, telephone, radio and cocktail cabinet.
Overleaf: The ultimate motor-car, The Bentley Mulsanne Turbo, named after the 200 mph straight on the Sarthe circuit in Northern France, where the Le Mans 24 hour race is run, and scene of famous Bentley victories.

2

3

1

2

coupé which started a trend which was to continue, for a convertible in the range. The year 1957 brought air conditioning, mainly for the American market, which demanded more power from the engine, provided by an increase in the compression ratio.

This eventually led to the 6,230 c.c. V8 which was to power all later models, growing bigger in the process. When the Cloud III appeared, the radiator was lower and four headlamps adopted as a prelude to the Silver Shadow, which sold in much larger numbers than any previous Rolls-Royce; in all 19,412 between 1965 and 1977, when the Silver Shadow II came on the market.

The Shadow incorporated more changes than any previous Rolls-Royce. It had a rear suspension layout bought from Citroen and modified, which allowed the car to rise and fall according to load. It was the first RR to employ disc brakes, long after everyone else had adopted them, because the engineers would not tolerate the squeal which discs were apt to make. The new car was faster and better in every way and cost £6,669 in 1965, with fuel consumption of 12 miles to the gallon.

The Silver Shadow II which followed in 1977 had another virtue;

3

4

(1) The massive Phantom VI. Since 1979, this model has been powered by the V8 unit used in the other models. (2) The Bentley Mulsanne (non-turbo version) with USA model headlamps. Except for the radiator shell, the car is identical to the Silver Spirit. (3) The Silver Shadow was the most successful of all the Rolls-Royce cars. Pictured here is the Shadow II introduced in 1977. This model was the first to be fitted with rack and pinion steering. (4, 5) The Corniche convertible has a hand-built two-door body by Mulliner Park Ward, and is somewhat more sporting in character.

5

rack and pinion steering, and was much improved in terms of ride and handling and much more of a driver's car. But in 1970 the company was in the hands of the receiver, and the car-making element was hived off into a separate and profitable company.

Later cars were developments of the Shadow but improvements continued. These were the two-door Corniche and Camargue, and then the 1980 Silver Spirit and the long wheel base Silver Spur. Steering, suspension and brakes have been improved over already excellent standards and the degree of refinement in the present-day Rolls-Royce is unique. There are bigger, faster and even more expensive cars in one-off form, but Rolls maintain their position by providing an unmatched product for its purpose.

In addition to the cars which almost anyone can buy (if they have the funds), there is still a model available only to royalty or heads of state for ceremonial purposes. This is the Phantom IV. The Phantom IV was designed for the British royal family in 1950 and is more than six feet high and 19 feet long. It has a straight-eight engine, the only one of its kind.

The Phantom IV, the biggest Rolls-Royce ever constructed, was based on the Wraith but was longer in order to take the bigger engine and to provide more room in the rear compartment. In 30 years, fewer than 20 Phantom IVs have been built to special order. The Phantom V

which was introduced in 1959 is less exclusive and in all 832 were made, all with coachbuilt bodies from one of the great names.

This model had the normal V8 engine as in the Cloud II and was produced until 1968. It used the four-speed Hydramatic automatic transmission and not the three-speed version which Rolls adopted with the Silver Shadow in 1965. The Phantom VI followed the Five and from 1979 used the bigger 6,750 c.c. V8 engine as in the late Shadow I and Shadow II.

The Phantom VI must be the world's most exclusive and expensive car, with a price tag, depending on degree of armour-plating, gold fittings and so on, of around £100,000. It must also be the only car to have two separate air-conditioning systems, one for the front and one for the rear compartment.

(1, 2) The two-door Camargue, designed by the Italian firm of Pininfarina, is produced in limited quantities and is one of the more exclusive cars in the range. Bodies are hand-built by Mulliner Park Ward. (3, 4) The

Silver Spirit is considered vastly superior to its predecessors in terms of ride and handling. It incorporates a large number of modifications over the Shadow II that it has supplanted.

(1) Despite inheriting many of the components of the Silver Shadow II, the Silver Spirit is much more than just a new body shape. Rear suspension has been completely re-designed to give a different meaning to the terms ride, handling and stability. (2) On its introduction, the styling of the Camargue attracted a degree of criticism. However, beneath the skin, the car is in the finest Rolls-Royce tradition. (3) The long wheelbase Silver Wraith Mark II. (4) The Bentley version of the two-door fixed head Corniche coupé.

3

4

—CHAPTER TEN—

Frequent magazine articles recount how many complete cow hides and how many Circassian walnut trees go into each and every Rolls-Royce interior, and it is curious that there should be so much emphasis on the superficial finish of the interior and so little said about the engineering excellence, which is the real distinction of the company's product.

Rolls-Royce now make many more cars than ever before and use many bought in components instead of producing almost every part in their own workshops. The standards of manufacture and testing, and the back-up research, are still to the same meticulous standards laid down by Henry Royce, to whom the term 'Good enough' was unknown.

In the works at Crewe there is a Latin inscription which translates roughly as: 'Whatever is rightly done, however humble, is noble', and the whole organisation which produces the motor-car is geared to do the best possible job without regard to saving time, money or effort, despite having to make a profit.

Connolly hides of the best quality are carefully matched, and the veneers from the Caucasus mountain walnut trees arranged to make a mirror image on each half of a picnic table or ashtray or whatever, but this is only the icing on the cake. Some of the veneers are applied over plastic mouldings, so that beauty is only skin deep, but it is produced by five coats of varnish, with rubbing-down between each application.

Enormous care is taken over the assembly of engines, with parts weighed and balanced before assembly, and then when put together are motored over for several hours and a sample run on a bench for 24 hours, even before the lengthy road-testing begins. The radiator shell was once of brass, then of German silver, but since the nineteen-thirties has been of stainless steel.

Anything bought from an outside supplier is rigorously tested before use, and every car has its own book in which a permanent record is made of any snags which develop in manufacture, and how they are resolved. This bears the customer's name, as they really do build 'your' car. The Rolls-Royce, although with a pressed-steel body, still has a chassis and great care is taken when body and chassis are joined with a machine which applies air pressure to ensure even spreading of the load and proper tightening of bolts.

Crewe is an amalgam of the best of the traditional and peculiarly Royce practices and the best that has been learned through modern investigation and research. Each car is run for 50 miles on a test-bed and then everything is tested—twice. Painting takes nearly as long as an old master, with washing, degreasing, priming, oven baking, more baking, sealing. This is before the body is married to the chassis.

When the car is complete and has been road-tested it goes back to the paint shop to be flatted again, resprayed, and put through the oven once more. It may even go back a second time if the inspectors are not

satisfied. It will be weeks before the car is approved and has done its 150 miles road test. Apart from this emphasis on the cosmetic side, continuous testing is undertaken to ensure that every component is reliable.

Many of the test rigs have been devised by Rolls-Royce themselves out of spare materials and parts at minimal expense, because they have to perform some particular job for which no ready-made machines exist. There is one which keeps the steering turning from lock to lock under load, to point of failure. The laboratory technians will discover cause of breakdown and there will be a modification to see that it does not happen again.

Gearboxes and rear axles are subjected to abuse never envisaged by the designer. The object of the test rigs is to reproduce what happens on the road, only speeded up so that they can make their discoveries in a much shorter time. Most parts are expected to run 250,000 miles without failure, which should ensure a life of 100,000 miles in service without problems.

When components on a prototype fail under 10,000 miles then a new rig is employed, and faults can be isolated and rectified much more quickly than by running cars on the road over big mileages, although this technique is used also.

Brakes and brake materials are also tested rigorously on a rig which

The Corniche was the first model to appear with the larger 6750 cc V8 engine and improved air-conditioning. The car uses the General Motors Hydramatic GM400 three-step automatic transmission with torque converter, and has a top speed of 120 mph. Originally it was available in both fixed and drophead form, but the former has now been discontinued, and is the more unusual of the two. Overleaf: An elegant and unusual Phantom I with projecting rear boot, soft top and removable side-screens. The anti-glare tinted glass screen is unusual on a car of this year and type. Note the red enamel filling on the Rolls-Royce emblem, coincidentally changed to black in the year of Henry Royce's death.

can measure temperatures, life, the effects of moisture or overheating and anything else the engineers might want to know. Before adopting disc brakes RR worked with Ferodo to find a squeal-free formula. Radiators are subjected to a water-test which varies the internal pressure to breaking point and water pumps are run until they fail.

There is also a torture-trailer which can be towed behind a car to impose all sorts of abnormal loads by electrical means, controlled from the towing car. Electrical components are looked at particularly closely, bearing in mind that Royce's origins were as a manufacture of electrical equipment, and the master's spirit lives on.

Even minor items such as tool retaining clips, are tested to destruction to find out just what is the best way to achieve a task. Water and smoke tests find out any body leaks, and engines have to endure being frozen and then be expected to start up easily. It's a hard life being part of a Rolls-Royce.

All car manufacturers use test rigs, but Rolls have some very individual ones to do with noise reduction. Spring dampers and shock absorbers are given a gruelling time, and even steel wheels hammered until they split in a way that could never occur in service. The reason for the fault is discovered, and a better wheel emerges.

Acknowledgements

The publishers would like to offer their special thanks
to Rolls-Royce Motors Limited, Crewe, for allowing photographic facilities at
the factory, and for the loan of current models.

Reproduction of Rolls-Royce Trademarks and Copyright material
is made with the kind permission of its owners.

Featuring the photography of Clive Friend FIIP.
Photographs also supplied by C.W. Hughes, Edward Eves, Nicky
Wright (Stratford Motor Museum and A.C.D. Museum) and
Autocar Magazine.

Research by Hanni Edmonds.

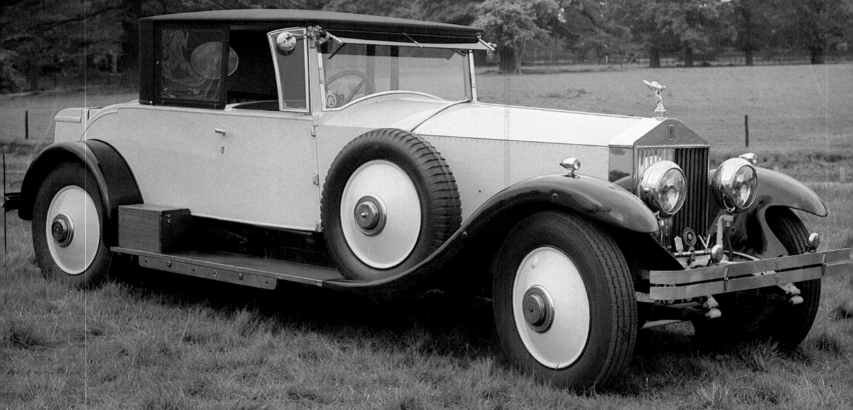

First English edition published by Colour Library International Ltd.
© 1982 Illustrations and text: Colour Library International Ltd., 99 Park Avenue, New York 10016
This edition is published by Crescent Books
Distributed by Crown Publishers, Inc.
h g f e d c b a
Colour separations by FER-CROM, Barcelona, Spain.
Display and text filmsetting by Focus Photoset, London, England.
Printed by Cayfosa and bound by Eurobinder - Barcelona (Spain)
Library of Congress Catalog Card No. 82-71201
All rights reserved
CRESCENT 1982